AN EXORCISM
of Angels

Stephanie M. Wytovich

**RAW DOG
SCREAMING
PRESS**

An Exorcism of Angels © 2015 by Stephanie M. Wytovich

Acknowledgments:

HWA Poetry Showcase, Vol. 1. "Monster, Me." Horror Writers Association. E-book. 2014.

Jamais Vu-Journal of Strange Among the Familiar. "Mermaids Can't Fall in Love." Post Mortem Press. Print. 2014.

Ugly Babies: An Anthology. "Baby No Name." James Ward Kirk Publishing. E-book. 2013.

Published by Raw Dog Screaming Press
Bowie, MD

First Edition

Cover illustration: Steven Archer
Book design: M. Garrow Bourke

ISBN: 978-1-935738-72-5
Library of Congress Control Number: 2015939341

Printed in the United States of America

www.RawDogScreaming.com

Contents

For You.
Always.

"Yes. That he was. No doubt of that. I swear he created five New Agonies, made just for me, and all made of love."
—Clive Barker, *Mister B. Gone*

This is my romance.
This is my horror.
This is my love letter to a broken heart.
To an angel and a demon.
And the Hell that they created.

—*Stephanie M. Wytovich*

ADDERALL

My attention is fine;
what I need is the consciousness,
the little blue pill that keeps me awake
that keeps me going—*fast, real fast*—
as I need the constant, the ever-moving,
the speed and the pitter-patter of my heart
threatening to jump out of my chest;

What I need is to trick my body
into being wired, into being alive,
even if it's only for a couple hours,
a temporary high that lets me breathe,
that lets me dance and smile and run,
run far and away, away from it all,
away from me, away from him;

Just a little blue pill that buys me
some hours, some sanity,
some courage to escape and I'll pay
it all back when I drink myself to sleep,
when I shut off the lights and peel
back my skin, shaking from the drop,
from the lows and the cold sweats,
from the regret and the inability
to make it permanent.

My attention is fine;
what I need is a reason to keep going,
to be able to hit fast-forward and not have a
reason or an excuse to stop.

He never answered me fast enough—that is, if he ever answered me at all—so I had to do something. What choice did I have? Was I supposed to just sit there and wait? Wait, like a dog? No, I gave up waiting years ago and when he showed up two months later, crying and sobbing at my front door, I smiled and embraced him, slid the needle into his skull, and the moment he started to come alive…

I ever so *gently* put him down.

ADVICE FROM A GHOST

I am not me. I am a stranger to myself. A figment. An imposter. Who I am now is a culmination of everything that I aspired not to be; a murderer, a thief, a monster. I have given and taken all that I can—I've broken hearts, stolen lives, and destroyed people who I've loved, people who I swore I'd protect—and I stand before you now, with but one piece of advice. Turn away. Don't look back. Run, run far and run fast. Disappear. Because he's not worth it, and by that, I mean that he is worth everything, everything that you cannot give him for he is fire, and he is burning and you will do nothing but put out his flames.

You will kill him, just like I killed him.
And then you will kill you.
Just like I killed me.

I extinguished all that I knew and all that I loved, and I am neither here nor there, not dead but not living. I am a messenger, a ghost, a scorned lover, a wife. And I am here to tell you that love will not kill you. It will erase you, make you a negative, an absence.

So walk away from it.
Close your eyes to it.
Swallow your pride and bury your lust.

Forget the delicate curl of his hair. The gentleness in his eyes. The way his lips caressed yours, or the way his hands trembled when you touched him. Remove him from your memory.

Because I can't…
I can't let him go.

There wasn't a lot left of her to give,
in fact, she worried if there was anything at all,
but when she kissed him, when she touched him
when she closed her eyes and shut off the pain,
a part of her started to come back—and it was
small, and it was weak—but it breathed inside of her,
filling her lungs with something that she hadn't
experienced in years—maybe something she'd never experienced
at all?—and it was hope, and it brought her to her knees because this hope,
this hope was worse than the pain, it gave meaning, gave happiness,
and built dreams, dreams that could be broken, that could
be destroyed, and while his lips lingered on hers, while
his hands trailed down her waist, she realized that each breath,
each moment he looked into her eyes was killing her a little more,
saving her a little more, and the seesaw of death and life fed her
heart a poison, a drug that only she could take, that only she could
handle, and if it killed her in the end, she'd at least die knowing
that she tried.

AN EXORCISM OF ANGELS

He was the moon and he pulled me towards him in the night;
I couldn't refuse him as our darkness and light fell into each other
like constellations in a Winter storm, turbulent but beautiful,
destructive but in happy madness.

I loved him, truly and without fault,
followed him with a blindness, with a trust that I had
never put in another before, for I was spelled,
enchanted by the why he sang to me, by the way he looked at me,
as if his lost soul had finally found its partner hiding in the
dustiest parts of this world.

Our demons met that night, and they laughed and they played,
cavorting in happy sin, but my angels were hesitant and they tried to
pull me away from the boy, away from his demons. I thought them jealous,
envious of my pleasure,
and I bid them farewell as I took the boy's hand and followed him
into the woods, skipping through snowflakes and kissing between
the harsh gusts of wind.

He told me there was a Hell inside him, a netherworld
that he couldn't escape, but his eyes were kind as he said it,
and I felt his pain, felt it like a thousand knives in my heart; I kissed
him then, kissed him knowing that I would make his Hell my own,
that I would take his pain and assuage his every sadness, my demons and his,
bound together in this vicious game of life, of love, two souls brought together
to find some light in all the dark.

Drug me. Fill me full of metal, fill me full of pills. Make the breaks and the aches go away, the nightmares and the shadows. I'm sick of wading through pain, of moving through anger, and I want the drill in my head, the taste of oxy on my tongue. It wasn't enough what you started with me, feeding my monster and setting her free. I can't close my eyes without seeing you, can't go to sleep without you next to me. Insomnia is in my veins, in my blood, and I just want to sleep, but I can't. Not without the rain, not without the glass. She's stronger now and I can't even feel myself anymore. I'm fading, falling and I can touch the fire that waits for me, waits with open arms.

I tried to fight, tried to say no, but it's her words on my lips, her whispers in my head. *Madness Madness Madness.* Some things never change and others never will and I've accepted that my demons don't play well with others, especially with yours. Yours don't have what it takes to sleep, to play, to eat with mine and you're only in my life now to provide my fix, her need. You woke her up again, again after I finally put her to sleep, and you, you started this, so you burn it up and you burn down, just get it inside me and make sure it lasts and don't worry if her voice sounds angry.

If she wanted to kill you, she would have.

BABY NO NAME

It wasn't a child.
To call it that would be *wrong*.
A child doesn't eat like that. Doesn't
drink from its eyes, smell from its mouth.
It walks on its hands—yes, its—I can't tell
the gender because there's nothing *there*. But
it sees with its fingers, and tastes all the sounds. It tells
me when I'm wrong—when I don't spend enough
time with it. Lectures me like an adult
with a voice that cracks and wheezes as if the
thing had smoked four packs a day for 20-something years
when it only crawled out of me three days ago.

I don't know where it's at now. It comes and goes as it pleases,
hates being in the light. It's probably under the couch
again, laughing like it does. It giggles at shadows, thinks
it's funny how they move. When I try to turn on the lamp,
it screams, so I don't. Better to stay in the dark. That way I don't
have to see it move.

One time, I tried to hold it. It burrowed into my cleavage,
cooing like the child it definitely was not. It looked at me with
its big green eyes and touched my face. It threw up water,
sneezed blood. Then it smiled a 200-toothed grin and kissed
my hand. I haven't held it since.

Beelzebub Over Gabriel

Gabriel knocked on my door last night,
the night of the Sabbath,
the night we first met,
but there were already demons in my head,
and I promised myself to Beelzebub
and that evening...
we wed.

BLACK WEDDING

She wore a wedding dress that felt like a mourning gown,
held a bouquet of flowers she wished were dead;
on the day when she was supposed to be happiest,
all she saw was the Devil in her bed.

Bleeding Beauty

I sat in the dark for a very long time that night. I lit a candle once, but then I thought better and blew it out. It was easier not to see anything, not even my hand in front of my face. I couldn't see the blood, couldn't see the tears. I felt them both, though. Hot and sticky. I imagined that I was a painting, and that I looked beautiful hanging on your wall.

BODY SNATCHING

Last night, I dreamt that I fell into a pile of bodies. The more I tried to breathe, the more the stench pulled me down, down into the pit, into the pool of broken limbs and decomposed flesh. I can still smell them, them with their maggots and their worms. The more I tried to escape, the harder the bodies held onto me with their yellowed skin and brittle nails. I didn't want to be there, didn't want to be next to the corpses, the cadavers that all had my eyes, my lips, my nose. I didn't want to sleep with them. They were mirrors that reflected what I felt, what I was. Death was inside of me and it met me in my dreams and when I woke up, I could still feel them. They were watching me in the shadows, waiting for me to fall back asleep.

Branded with Blasphemy

Serpents rode my tongue,
swam inside my mouth and it was all I could do
to pretend that they weren't slithering down my throat,
filling my lungs with venom, my voice box with
whispers, whispers that made me lie, that made me sin. I spoke
through hisses, laughed at the sacrilege that kissed
my lips and when they pushed the stake against my cheek,
I laughed at the cross embedded in my flesh and spat snakes
at their feet.

BRIDGES IN HER MIND

She built bridges in her head to keep him out, to confuse him every time he tried to get to her. They moved inside her mind: upside-down, sideways, diagonally, and they knew him by name, by face, by touch, and he'd scream for her, beg for her, pleading for her to let him back in, but she'd shut him out, shut him up inside her head, lost in a tunnel, in a maze that he'd never escape because it was her labyrinth of memories and she was the only one who knew how to get out.

He was a saint—at least in her eyes—but she knew
he had to die in order for others to see her point-of-view,
in order for others to see the God in him, and the virgin
in her. She cut him, sliced him up in little pieces and wrapped
him carefully, boxing him up and leaving him at the church's
door. She washed her knives in holy water, prayed for his
deliverance. It would take time, but eventually they'd see. Murder
might be old testament, but knives were the new crucifixion.

CHAMOMILE TEARDROPS

Someone once told her that crying was good for insomnia, so she started to drink her tears. They tasted like hot chamomile tea on a cold night, and they put her to sleep like no pill ever could. She stopped taking her medicine, and instead, kept finding reasons to cry. Every night she'd play back memories, rewind the stories in her head, reliving, remembering. It was a one-act suicide play. She didn't even realize it when she started to drown. She was finally asleep and the waves felt good.

Coffee and Cigarettes

I bought him a cup of coffee and a pack of cigarettes, told him I loved him and then drove away, my sunglasses covering my red-rimmed eyes soiled with pain. The low settled in quick, quicker than any time before, and I died on my way home, died knowing that this time, I wasn't coming back. That there would be no more second chances. That we'd both run out of excuses to give.

COUNTING BLESSINGS

They didn't burn my wings;
they just cut them off and hung
them on the wall like a trophy,
like a prize. In a way, I feel blessed that
Wrath still lets me look at them,
lets me remember what it felt like to fly,
to stretch out my feathers and take the clouds,
to take the Heavens, and it's because of that
that blissful memory of freedom, of escape, that
I know he's doing it, doing it to remind me that good
doesn't always win, and that even the best of angels
can fall when they're shot out of the sky.

He was my church
and I happily dropped to my knees for him
and no matter my penance,
I always did as I was told.

CYCLE OF INCUBI

Sometimes it's not enough to wake up screaming in the middle of the night, to hear your voice crack and shatter while you gasp for air, struggling, trying, pretending everything is okay, that you're not still in there, the nightmare, the reoccurrence, the always happening. There are some dreams that you can't wake up from, some stories that you can't un-hear, and when the lights go out, when the moon swallows the sun, the darkness brings them all to life, brings them all swarming front and center in a mind that can't hide from the memories that are locked within, that are trapped and beating down the door to get free.

So let me kill you,
Let me make it end...

Because sometimes it's not enough to ask for forgiveness, to repent and pray, to fall down on your knees before you close your eyes and whisper your lover's name, until you cry just one more tear. See, there's no escaping the poison that flows through your synapses, the fear that controls the regret pressed inside your head, inside your heart. There are some things that can't be forgotten, that need to be remembered, and when you fall asleep at night and see his face, it's not a punishment. It's a form of penance. One terror a day, every day, until death, your death.

So let me kill you now,
Please, just let me make it end...

When I saw him standing there, I knew it was going to end badly, and when he stared at me with those big brown eyes, it was as if he was sizing me up to eat me. I didn't have a chance at surviving him, and I knew this, knew it right from the start. And maybe part of me wanted to die, but another part of me hoped he wouldn't kill me, hoped that I was wrong.

DAYMARES

I hear people brag all the time about how they never sleep and it makes me want to scream because I can't even measure the amount of sleep I've had. My days, weeks, and months all run together, all blur in some surrealist mess, and the circles under my eyes hold stories and heartbreak and I can't even remember why they're there. It feels like an eternity since I've dreamed, since I've had a chance to close my eyes and not be afraid of what's waiting for me behind them, of what's lurking in my head, and part of me knows it's you—that it's always been you—and part of me is happy not finding out for sure.

Dear -

The light on my desk is flickering and I'm drinking from a jug of wine, smoking half-broken cigarettes as I hang out my bedroom window, too obsessed to walk away from the words that I need to put on paper so I don't forget a single moment, a single memory of that winter. The seasons have changed since I've seen you last but there is still snow in my heart, still ice in my eyes and no matter how many blankets I cover myself in, I can't shake the cold that wraps itself around my shoulders since you walked away that January night.

I play piano sometimes when I try to start my day, when I try to rekindle something of my past, but my music all sounds haunted now, plagued by the days when we'd sit at the keys together, your hands on mine, teaching me how to play. I remember feeling alive then, feeling that maybe it was okay to let myself feel if I had someone there to play away my melancholy, to drink pleasure against my pain. Love became something that I started to believe in again, something that I thought I could see when you sang me to sleep at night, but love is an obsession, and obsession doesn't work when only one person's heart is beating.

And yet months later that light is still flickering and my jug is almost empty and there are ashes in my hair. I've forgotten my song, and my heart is somewhere in this typewriter, somewhere in between these keys, and I keep trying to find myself—the self I swore I'd never lose again—but every time I start to find her, she's still attached to memories of Christmas, to a kiss that shouldn't have happened, to a heart that no longer knows how to love.

DEMONS FOR LOVERS

I used to know a boy who refused to let go of his demons—his angels—and as a result they tore the wings from his back and laughed as he bled, broken and screaming on his bedroom floor. His suffering attracted them, fueled them, and eventually, he, out of desperation, out of masochism, grew to love them, need them, depend on them. They became an entity which he could not live without, so he'd wake up in the morning and digest them, inhale them, drink them, cut them, become them and no matter what I did, no matter what I tried to do, I couldn't save the soul within, couldn't save the boy within, and by the time I ripped off my own wings to be with him, they had already swallowed him whole.

Diet

I broke my alarm clock this morning
and I'm out of coffee and the only thing I have to drink
in my fridge is a jug of Carlo Rossi; I can't remember
the last time I went shopping for food, but I have enough
cigarettes and booze to get me through the next couple
of days and as long as I can stay sober enough to write,
I should be fine.

DISEASED DAMSEL

He said I was a disease
and he was right.
I'd been poisoning him
since the day we met and if
fate happens to turn out to be
the capricious whore that
I know she is, she'll let him die with
his mouth open, so very close to screaming,
but so very much unable to.

Drowning Him

He's the whiskey on my lips, the blood on my fingertips and when I close my eyes, when I listen real hard, it takes everything inside of me not to smile. His memory used to bother me, used to dig down deep inside my chest and scratch at my heart, but now when I feel him, it's nothing but a reminder of how I survived—beaten, broken, and half-mad—but still, a survivor.

I'm alive and breathing—not well—but I'm moving, walking on weary legs stumbling over past regrets but I keep standing up, I keep moving forward, because I'm hard to kill even when I'm already dead, and if half the world goes black and half the world goes white, it won't be me that gets buried in the darkness because the darkness lives and thrives and breeds inside of me. His solitude brings me peace, his isolation gives me sanity, and yet to me, he's already been dead. The plague in my head decided days ago that it was time for him to leave, time for him to go.

And now I sit and I wonder and I think, think, think about love, about pain, about lust and death and when his face comes to my mind, rippling in the black waters of my brain, I know that in time those brown eyes will lose their hold on me, will lose their ability to make me remember, to make me forget, and so when I see his face in the lake in my head, I take a deep breath and push him back under, suffocating whatever pieces of him keep trying to resurrect.

EATEN BY SHADOWS

He only loved her when the stars came out, when the sun hid behind the clouds and the night blanketed the sky. She knew she wasn't sunshine, but she also knew she could be...if someone gave her the chance, the opportunity. Her heart was big, it was just encased in stone, always loved from afar or just never loved much at all. So she'd wait, wait until the darkness came and swallowed her big brown eyes, until the blackness ate away her smile and stole the shine from her auburn hair. And then when he couldn't see her anymore—when she'd become just a shadow—she knew she'd be good enough. She knew he'd want her then.

Eclipse

Your eyes are an eclipse,
two black holes that
stare straight through me and
I'm not sure when it started,
but I know that before when I looked at you,
I used to see stars.

EMBRACING HER DARKNESS

There's no greater feeling than coming back alive
after you've been dead for so long;
So fuck the seraph,
I'll be manic with the beast if I get to feel like this.

There's an empty suitcase on my bed but I haven't decided what I want to do with it yet; the idea of packing up my life and taking it with me makes me feel trapped, makes me feel sick, and there's a part of me that wants to leave, leave with it full of nothing, because nothing means freedom, means a new beginning, a new life. I can fill that suitcase full of smiles instead of carrying around years of abuse, of heartbreak, of tears. I want to throw away my photo albums, erase the songs in my head, remove the phantom touch you left on my skin; I want nothing so I can have everything: fresh cities with fresh faces, different time zones and languages I don't understand.

I see a girl on the train tracks.
Hear a whistle in the air.

She has my eyes, my cheeks, my hair and she's holding a sign that says "Anywhere, Anywhere but Here" and there's something familiar about the way she moves, about how she walks towards the train, the train that isn't stopping, that isn't slowing down. I see her lips moving, reciting prayer, singing song, and I wonder what she's saying, what she's whispering to the world, and I question if the universe hears her, if it's responding back.

And now my suitcase is on the train tracks.
A second whistle hits the air.

She turns her head and looks at me, smiles and closes her eyes. The sign drops to the ground and she's still smiling, smiling as she embraces the train. My scream is lodged in my throat and I'm crying, crying, can't stop crying, but there's no body on the tracks, no blood on the soil. Like a ghost, she left as quickly as she came, drifting through days, through hours, through minutes, but her suitcase—my suitcase—is still there, shoved up against the tracks, the locks busted and swinging from impact.

Inside it is a sign.

A sign that says "Anywhere, Anywhere but Here."

The Tarot always read in his favor,
never in mine, and it was as if the deck was
stacked with swords,
out of balance with growing negativity,
with impending regret,
and each time I flipped a card,
I felt my skin shriek as the point of the blade
dug in a little further, always reminding me
how he made me bleed—
he, that liar, that cheat, that thief,
the one who stole my heart from my chest,
the heart that I was so hesitant to give,
and yet our pattern was simple,
never wavering, concrete in its stubborn ways
for I always went back to him
ever entranced as the stars predicted,
locked in a cycle of despair,
in a darkness bred out of love.

ETERNAL WINTER

Inside her was a frozen wasteland
and her organs were snowballs,
her veins shards of ice. When she blinked,
crystals fell from her eyelashes,
and her lips were stitched together
in a permanent sadness.
After him,
everything went white and winter,
desolate and cold.
He murdered her summer days
and spring afternoons, her daffodils
and happy memories. There was no
coming back from the dead,
no seasonal rebirth,
and nothing can grow
inside her now, not love, not a child
and there's nothing left but sleet in her throat,
and snowflakes in her stomach,
and she'll never be warm again.

Ever Unclean

I begged him to baptize me,
to wash it all away, to make me a blank slate,
an unmarked woman that no one had ever seen,
ever branded, ever fucked, but he laughed, laughed
at my pleas as he liked that I was unclean, that I had been
used, abused, that I was broken and shattered. He
said it gave me character, gave me something to think about,
someone to blame, and that I should take that anger,
that malice, and use it to my advantage for my sins against others
were no longer to be punished, but celebrated, and my filth
was now a halo, one he said I should wear with pride.

FALLEN

I gave up my wings for him,
fell from the sky and turned
on the clock to mortality. I
thought he was perfect but the
truth of it was:
not every angel has wings,
and there's a reason why
Hell exists.

Femme Fatale

Before I'd go and see him, I'd take off my halo and remove my wings, exchange them for fishnet stockings and a black and red corset. I liked the way they looked against my porcelain skin and part of me knew that when he saw me, that he'd never be able to tell, that he'd never know who or what I really was. For a while it worked out fine—we'd laugh, we'd drink, we'd fuck—but then I sensed him starting to wonder, starting to feel something, something that seemed an awful lot like love. But that's a game that I learned long ago to quit playing and the second someone tries to stick Cupid's arrow in me, is the second I walk away.

FILL HER FULL OF NIGHTMARES

Locked away in her head, the girl only hungered, only yearned for one thing: the needle. She wanted the rush of fire in her veins, the constant ringing in her ears, and when it became too much, she wanted the collapse, the drug-induced coma that would let her sleep for days, that would lock her in her nightmares and make her face them head-on instead of letting her run away, instead of letting her hide, hide inside her head.

One prick.
Two prick.
Three prick, four.

She fantasized about it for hours, days, weeks, but all she ever saw was the little cup of pills that they slipped through the metal-framed hole in her door and—honestly—those slices of hell did nothing, nothing! They cleared her mind, invited new monsters, monsters that were worse than the old ones, and when they realized she stopped taking them, when they found them stitched inside her mattress, stuffed inside her pillow case, ground up and broken on the floor, they all made a decision to personally make sure she took them.

Five pricks.
Six pricks.
Seven pricks, more!

They strapped her to the bed, her wrists red-raw from the restraints. She heard the steady drip-drop of the IV and her heart danced furiously in her chest. The orderlies slapped her arm—*c'mon body, give them that big blue vein*—and stabbed her full of medicine, filled her full of demons. Her body shook, jackhammering in the bed, and as her eyes rolled back, as the lights began to dim, to flutter, to fade, she smiled. Smiled because she was going home. Smiled because now she could finally fight.

I woke up amongst the flames,
amongst the screaming and the blood,
my lips chapped and dry, my skin burned and flaking,
and there was a flower painted on my chest,
a group of wilted petals that I'd gotten to know well;
the boy, he traced them in my ashes every morning before I woke up
as an apology for bringing me here, as a sign that he was sorry for what he
put me through, but the thing about ashes is that they're proof of destruction
and there weren't enough roses that could heal what had become of my soul
as I, myself, was a bouquet of death, my sins blossoming every afternoon
when the Devil called my name.

FORGET-ME-NOTS

It was hard to place blame on a situation where blame was the least of their worries, and time—no matter how much had passed—couldn't fix their wounds, even though at some points, existence became bearable again; she could walk around with a smile on her face despite the way hurt latched its teeth into her heart, and he could laugh, could eat, drink, fuck, without caring how it affected her, how it affected him, but it wasn't until the moment when the two of them went to sleep at night, when the lights went out and the only eyes on them—staring into them—were their own, that they thought of each other, somewhere deep between the shadows and the memories, in that place where they could love each other without fear, without shame, without consequence, just as two souls who were destined for each other, by each other, should, but were unable to.

The more I wore
his bruises,
the harder it became
to convince myself
that
God
still
cared

GAMBLING WITH THE FATES

Past.

Present.

Future.

No matter which one you talk to, she's going to fuck you in the end, but maybe that's the beauty of the gamble. You're taking a chance at the lesser of three evils, choosing between a shot gun to the face, a slow and steady poisoning, or a knife right in the back. Past, now she brings the pain; full of nothing but would-haves and could-haves, regrets and remorse. If her memories don't kill you, the stagnant pull of Present will. She's the constant reminder that nothing worked out like you wanted it to, that everyone left, that everyone died, and if she doesn't make you fold your cards, then you can always turn to Future. Christ knows at least there's death waiting for you there.

Ghost

He called her ghost because she came and went without
rhyme or reason and she was neither gone nor present. She
existed as much as she knew how to, and when he'd reach out,
sometimes she'd let him touch her, but most of the time
all she gave him was an idea of who she really was.

GIFT OF ROSES

He knew I liked to be surrounded by roses,
that they made me feel loved,
made me feel special,
so when he stabbed me that day,
that day it all fell apart,
he put the stem through my neck,
knowing that my blood would brighten the petals,
that it would kill me, just as I'd killed his
love when I left.

Good Morning, Good Night

There are no good mornings, no good nights, no signs of want or need. In my days that turn into weeks, that turn into months, there is only static, a constant state of being where no one talks, no one listens. My throat is dry, bare, and I can't cough out the cobwebs that climb my throat, and I probably wouldn't even try if you asked me, even if you begged, because my good mornings died long ago, and then you slaughtered my good nights before they could exist. I didn't get to enjoy the moments where I should have been happy. With you, everything went straight to darkness and I didn't even get a light for you to kill.

GROWING SINS

She woke up and went to her garden every morning at 5:30 a.m., sat down and prayed, and then screamed till the sun came up. When her voice went hoarse, when it cracked and she wheezed, she wrote her sins on separate pieces of paper and shoved them into the ground—to give them a voice! to give them a life!— all the while crying that they were worth it, that she didn't regret them at all.

Wrath *because of him.*
Lust *because of him.*
Pride *because of him.*
Envy *because of him.*
Greed *because of him.*
Sloth *because of him.*
Gluttony *because of him.*

They grew like weeds, spreading through dawn, infecting the sky with heavy blooms of yellows and reds. The girl lifted her head and sang to the heavens, thanking God for this wonderful gift—for this beautiful miracle!—as she plucked each flower and put their petals in a jar. She kept her wickedness close, stocked her pantry with debauchery. She'd repent again tomorrow, as soon as the Devil woke her up.

Halo of Horns

There's a ritual to this,
this, her striptease of sin,
for this angel is still taking off her halo,
still sharpening her horns,
and there's something erotic about the wait,
about watching her slide out of her wings
because underneath all that innocence
is a patient devil
and when she beckons you,
be ready to answer,
yes, dear lover, be ready to *scream.*

HE CALLED HER *LITTLE PSYCHO*

He called her *Little Psycho*, but he didn't really know what he was saying. There was no way he could tell what she was thinking, what she was planning, what was she was envisioning every time she looked at him, every time his words made her dig the knife a little deeper into her thighs. Little Psycho wasn't angry, she was just sick of being hurt, tired of being let down, of being second to the bottle, second to the drugs, and when the silence started to scream, when his tongue started to bite, *Little Psycho* stopped being sad and decided to start earning her name, to start living up to the person who he thought she was but didn't know she actually could be.

Ha.

      Ha.

Ha.

But *Little Psycho* didn't know that *Hysteria* lived within her. Didn't know that when pushed, that she still had some fight left in her, some anger that she'd never even explored. It wasn't until he came at her, raging and riding his high, that she knew she could kill him if she had too, that she could kill him even if she didn't. The more she tried to believe in love, the more she realized it didn't exist. Not for her. Not this time around.

Ha.

      Ha.

Ha.

So she laughed, and she laughed until tears rolled down her cheeks, until her stomach hurt from the giggles, cramped from the fun. *Little Psycho* reveled in the moment as she drank from the bottle, as she took a hit from the smoke blanketing the room. She removed the knife from her boot, walked towards him—him, strung out and oblivious, ignorant to a different type of high, a better type of drug. *Little Psycho* would earn her name fair and square. And this time, she'd wear the brand with pride.

He'll Never be Able to Love Her

There is an exquisite pleasure
in loving someone
who doesn't love you back and it fills
the body—fills the heart—
full of everything and nothing
at the same time. It's a slow death,
a confusing life and there's a strangeness
about it because it can't be understood;
you're repulsed but you're attracted, you're
in love but you're in hate and in the end
you're powerless because you like the
challenge. It gives you something
to work for, something to try and change.

HIS LOVE IS AN ASYLUM

Trapped in her cell, a cell with white walls, no windows and a door that was locked from the outside-in, she took a breath, a breath that caused her to die a thousand deaths, dream a million dreams, and still—at the end of it—love stood there, *he* stood there, always waiting at the end of every moment, every nightmare, crawling, screaming, ripping her apart, tearing at her head, at her heart, at her flesh, and he was inside of her, a part of her, and no matter what she did, no matter how many times she banged her head against the walls, no matter how many times she painted them red with her blood and tore the paint off with her nails, there he was. Eternally there. In the shadows, in the light, in the medicine and sobriety.

He was there.

There.

There.

There.

Always fucking there.

Honesty Hides in Her Reflection

She brushed her hair in slow strokes and fought her reflection in the mirror. This wasn't the girl who she fought so hard to bring back to life, the one who she picked up off her bedroom floor covered in blood and tears, saliva and bruises, the one left drowning in heartache and lies. No, this wasn't the girl who promised that she wouldn't let things get bad again, the one who swore that she wouldn't let herself become vulnerable to the point where her pain wore plain on her face.

This wasn't her, not really anyways. That person was gone, lost somewhere between the liquor and the drugs, and the person who stared back at her, the person who met her eyes and challenged her stare was much, much worse. She was pale and ashen, broken in spirit, with shadows under her eyes, and beneath her cheekbones, there were monsters, monsters that fought under her skin, ripping, tearing, and clawing their way out, and sometimes the mirror cracked around her neck, a silver slit that separated her from the body that betrayed everything she knew.

Yes, on the outside she looked quite normal, almost just like every other girl—bright, accomplished, warm and full of smiles—but on the inside there was something missing, something very wrong and not okay, and she saw it every time she looked in the mirror, every time she watched her reflection kill herself a little more.

HOW TO DESTROY AN ANGEL

If I were to be portrayed as an angel, I'd have black wings and be unable to fly. I've done things, horrible things, and there's ash on my hands from falling from the clouds. I didn't think that I'd ever be able to leave, that I'd ever have the chance to get away, but I was wrong, and now I'm paying for it. No one believes you when you say that you're an angel who fell in love with the Devil, because no one thinks it's possible. No one so good could fall so far, no one so pure could welcome a permanent stain on their conscience, but no amount of praying, no amount of tears could prevent me from believing that there was something more to him than darkness, from reminding myself that he was once an angel, too. And now there's blood on my thighs, and my bones have been ripped from my back, some shattered, some plucked out like ivory knives thrust in the back of God. My punishment is waiting, waiting to see if the Devil will keep his word, waiting to see if he'll come back for me, me, whose biggest sin was always having too much faith.

The day was cold and wet and her tears were frozen to her lips like rough-cut diamonds and when she tried to yell for him, her lips stuck together even though they tried desperately to rip apart, and they bled and they bled and the crimson crept into her mouth soaking her tongue with copper and hurt and she choked and cried and her tears continued to freeze until her eyes turned to ice, turned to crystal, and all she could do was stare at him and watch him walk away.

I'LL TAKE HELL OVER HIM

At least when I was in Hell things made sense; at least when I burned,
it was by my own hand. But things are different now, you changed the game,
changed the sin, and I don't know how to act, and I don't know how to
kill, how to cry. The Devil wasn't cruel like you, he was honest in his hate,
straightforward with his punishments. He only brought the pain when I
deserved it. You brought it whether I earned it or not.

I've been a little confused,
a little distracted, breathing in the morning
and wheezing out the night. I shut my brain
off to normal, and welcomed in the madness,
the crazy talk, the insanity of everyday life,
of love, of hate, an eclipse of energy, of soul, of
mind, and I died for seconds, for minutes, for hours,
lost in the transit of beautiful cacophony, of blissful chaos
where I swam through the galaxies of broken dreams
and lost hearts, thinking about you, about us, about me
and how I've drowned in your sadness for too many nights,
holding you, embracing your demons, trying to be strong
enough for the both of us, but when the moon turns off
and the sun opens her eyes, the truth is bright and vibrant,
blinding me with the harsh reality of a woman's pain
who can't help the man she adores because he doesn't
remember how to love.

I'LL NEVER *REALLY* FORGET HOW TO DIE

Sometimes—on very few occasions—I forget what it feels like
to die, but never mind you, friend. There's no reason to worry,
not about little old me. You see, I have a stockpile of death inside
this broken body and when I move my bones crack, and when I love
my heart bleeds and even in those moments when I smile through
the pain, when I pretend that there's a chance that the life I was supposed
to live still exists, I know deep down inside that there's nothing but ashes,
nothing but soot in my lungs. No real part of me changes, I'm as stagnant
and consistent as they come, and if I trick you with my laughter, or
kiss you into confusion, you only have yourself to blame for I am a
monster, a creature who thrives in her pain.

I'm Doing Fine

He asked me how my day was
and I lied and said it was fine,
but really, there's been a lot of sitting
and staring
and sleeping
and I'm wondering if there's an easy way to do this,
to see him again without seeing him,
because being with him hurts
no matter how much it makes me happy
so fine isn't accurate
fine is a lie
what I am is dying
slowly
in your memory,
in leftover pictures of us
and when I wake up in the morning
there's no song in my heart
no story in my head
there's only tear drops on my pillow
and a wish that didn't come true
no matter how many nights I've stayed
up till 11:11,
no matter how many shooting stars I've caught
and given your name
it always ends in disappointment,
in you leaving
and me watching you walk away

JACK DANIELS FOR BREAKFAST

I keep a bottle of Jack under my bed for all those days that I keep waking up, for all those moments when my sobs get too loud. I use my coffee cup sometimes, but I usually drink straight from the bottle. I just have to make sure my eyes are closed so I can't see my reflection, so I can't change my mind. It hurts less each time I swallow, hurts more each time I go numb, and the Devil is underneath my covers, urging me to take another shot. I keep thinking that the pain in my chest is temporary, but it never seems to go away, and his whispers keep getting louder. *Bottoms up. Cheers to us. Just one more.* And now I can't remember a time when he wasn't there, a time when I could think for myself. I don't know how long it's been, but I know I haven't been sober in months. Whether I'm awake or sleeping, I'm content being drunk.

I kept telling him to stop it, kept begging him to quit. But he wouldn't. He called me by her name one too many times, so many in fact that I started to taste her on my lips, feel her moving in my head. When I looked in the mirror, my eyes were her shade of brown, and there was no denying that my clothes fit differently as my body started to change. I had to kill her. I had no other choice. She was everywhere—inside of me, inside of him—and I refused to share, refused to let her win, and jealously is just another name for manslaughter, a different way of protecting what's yours.

JOIN ME FOR A DRINK

Sit down.
Take a moment and breathe.
I won't keep you long,
I don't need to.

Here, have a drink.
It will be easier that way
easier for you,
easier for me.

Now talk to me.
Tell me your sins,
and maybe I'll tell you mine.
Show and tell, my pet
quid pro quo,
even angels need to
eat.

Judgment Day

I knew I wasn't good anymore when I decided that I wanted him dead, and not just dead, but damned and swollen beneath the ground, his body six feet under, his soul writhing in Hell. My halo splintered and it broke into horns, my feathers molted and blew away. I stood there, a shadow of who I used to be, an angel, a guardian, an innocent, but that all changed the night I met him, and now instead of white, I'm colored black with tar, with dirt, with sin, and my ability to forgive, to believe in the greater good is gone. I traded in my wings for a stab at revenge, and no matter what the cost, I've lost more than I care to imagine, and no amount of judgment can change my mind. I may have become a fallen, but I can guarantee you, I'll never try to fly again.

JUSTIFIABLE PUNISHMENT

The days were cold and the nights were worse, and no matter how many times I closed my eyes—when I opened them—it was still snowing, still freezing. The ice in the air had sealed my lips, prevented me from screaming, from begging, pleading, but the truth of the circle was that I belonged here, here among the blasphemers, the sodomites and usurers. Trapped in the valley of sand, I was bound and condemned by my tongue, and that's why the Devil took it when he left me here to forever sink into the ground.

When I close my eyes at night,
I feel the monster in my chest;
she's still breathing—
still beating after all these years.

KEEPING YOU ALIVE

It's 10 a.m. and I smell like cigarettes, smell like rain and I've been standing in the dark waiting for it to tell me something, anything other than that I'm wrong, wrong about the taste of wine on my tongue, about the boy I left in the country that day, that day I drove away from love, from trust, from everything I thought I knew, wrong about sleeping in, about cutting working, cutting class, about feeling more like myself than I ever did before, and now I'm against this wall, writing, writing on doors, on scraps of papers, on *me* because it's the only way I have to find him, the only way to keep his memory alive.

Kerosene

He made me drink the kerosene so he could burn my wings from the inside out, but the joke was on him. Stripped of my sainthood, I was already unable to go home and now all I had to look forward to was the fuel, the slow death, the steady life, and no matter how hard I flapped my arms, it wasn't the same. My wings were gone, and without them, so was I.

KICKING THE HABIT

The first time I tried sin it was by accident. I didn't want to do it, but *everyone* was doing it and I have a hard time saying no. It was supposed to be just a one-time thing, but he kept pushing me to do it, kept begging me with those big brown eyes. I tried to resist—not hard, but I did try—but truth be told, I would have done anything for him—anything to him—if I thought it would make him love me. But that's the tricky part about sin. It doesn't get you where you want to go, but once you start, it feels too good to stop, and stopping wasn't something I was ready to do. Not then.

But now...

Now things have changed, and they've changed in a way that I didn't see coming—that I should have seen coming, but didn't— because there's no trusting an addict. An addict will always pick themselves over you, no matter the price, no matter the sin, and this game that I'm playing isn't one I'm going to win, not if I keep playing it with you.

AN EXORCISM

Kidnapping the Devil

I've been wrong about a lot in my life, but I was never more wrong about anything, or anyone, than you. Yes, I was enticed by your darkness; that I will admit. I wanted to save you, wanted to keep you from drowning, but you pulled me down, filled my lungs with water. I thought that love was the answer to everything, but love has no place inside of you. You're a rejection slip, a reflection, a hologram of a person. I don't know *what* I fell in love with that night—an apparition? a vision?—but whatever it was, it wasn't human and I was too foolish, too young, too innocent to see the big picture because when you spoke to me, I heard music play in my soul, I felt flowers bloom in my heart. At 24, I was seduced by a man who wasn't a man; by a darkness that wasn't a darkness. I wasn't struggling with Hell. I was trying to salvage what was left of its creator.

KISS ME DEAD

He was every poem that I wanted to write,
every story that I wanted to read,
and yet there I was, dying on the kitchen floor,
unsure of how I got there,
unable to take the knife out of my chest.

I remember words, bad words, and they were yelled
and then the chairs were against the wall,
the table turned over, the dishes broken, shattered
on the dining room floor.

It hurt to breathe and I started to do it less and less but
he didn't stop screaming, didn't stop throwing his
fists against my face. The knife was new, though,
I never saw that one coming, but I should have, battered
and brainwashed as I was.

But even with its metal tip slashing my flesh,
it still hurt less than his kiss, the kiss that he kept
planting on my lips as he repeated how sorry he was,
as he begged me not to die.

And perhaps I wouldn't have if he hadn't kissed me,
but there are some pains that are too great,
some lies that no woman can live through,
no matter how strong she thinks she is.

When I first met Lazarus, she told me that she wanted to die. She even had it all planned out, was convinced that this time it would work. I knew it was a sin, and I warned her—*Christ, did I warn her*—but she wouldn't listen to me. She kept talking about some faraway place where sin didn't matter, and I told her that that was impossible, that no place like that existed, that we were all accountable for our sins at one time or another, but she insisted. Said she talked to some wise man, some prophet. I told her that no man of God would tempt her soul away, and she laughed, said she already sold it, but that God kept bringing her back, kept keeping her away.

LEARNING WHEN TO LET GO

I've never understood how some women can't let go,
how they'd spend their nights constantly dying, crying, living with pain
over what could have been,
what wasn't, and what never would be,
for when a man breaks my heart,
I no longer look at him as a man,
and that makes it easier to let go,
to let my brothers and sisters
assuage my pain with screams,
to let my hurt be washed away
as I watch the show,
the castration tango,
the mutilation rag.

Light Them, Burn Them

I don't believe in love,
don't believe that being good will land you in Heaven,
so I play with fire,
light lots of matches,
and I watch people and places burn,
burn slow and burn fast,
and I dance in their wreckage
as the earth cries between my legs,
its vibrations like soft lullabies
fucking me to sleep.

LITTLE STITCHES OF SLEEP

All my life, I complained that I was tired, exhausted, worn-out. I wanted to be able to lay down, I wanted to be able to close my eyes, to fade into my nightmares, my dreams that were kinder than the life that I lived. But I couldn't. Not until I met him: the dream-weaver, the sleep doctor. And I begged him to help me, pleaded with him to cure me, to make the insomnia, to make the daylight go away. He laughed as he touched my eyes and his flesh was hard, grainy as if it were made of sand, a human beach. And then I was falling, falling, falling deeper and deeper until all I saw was blackness and all I heard was static, static as the years passed like days, as the days passed like seconds. When I first saw light, it was through sleep-crusted eyelids, crisscrossed with stitches, stapled shut to sleep so I would never be tired again because with no way to open my eyes, all I could do was rest.

Every day is a new beginning, a new chance for opportunity, or so they promised me, but they weren't around after I destroyed everything, after I blew up the world. I was sick of the scriptures, disgusted by the hymns, and I tried—*honestly*—I really did what I could, but the more good I put out in life, the more bad it threw back at me, and part of me started to wonder if this was all some joke, if religion was just a scare tactic that was instilled in my head as a little girl to make me behave, but I'm not a little girl anymore, and no man— *not once*—has ever tried to save me, has ever provided me with anything but a knife in my back. It took Peter three times to deny God, but it will only take me once, because what's a girl to do when everything she believes in is a lie? When everyone she loves turns out to be a monster?

Well, she builds an ark of course.
And then she burns everything and everyone that should have gone on it.

LOST INSIDE

There was silence in her world
but screaming in her head
and the voices just kept yelling,
you're dead
you're dead
you're dead.

Only heartbreak slept on his tongue, only sadness kissed her at night. When he touched her, it was with shadows, allowing the disease of despair to move within her, a subtle puppeteer controlling her every move. There were times when she wasn't clawing at her bed sheets, when she wasn't pulling out her hair, but there were more times when she was climbing walls where week-old scratch marks lined the headboard and blood painted the splintered frame.

Yet she still slept with the boy every night, letting him drain her, letting him have her and she told herself that one day it wouldn't be like this, that one day she wouldn't need the fantasy that she'd built up in her head, that he wasn't just darkness, that the nails were coming loose, that the rust was fading fast, that it wasn't something darker underneath, but even then she knew she was lying to herself. The bite marks on her back, the raw, reddened skin on her wrists told her that. And one of those times when he pulled out the knife, when he tied her down to the floor, it wasn't going to be in jest, it wasn't going to be for intimidation. He would kill her. Of that she was certain. And of that, she didn't care.

MERMAIDS CAN'T FALL IN LOVE

I wanted to be the kind of girl that brought beauty into his life, but instead, I'm the kind of girl that brings stingrays and sea monsters, electric eels and seaweed skin. I wanted to believe that I could bring him to surface, that I could lay him down on the sand and kiss him back to life, but the only activity that I'm good at is drowning, and even though he was different, and even though I saw something in his eyes, something behind the dark blue tidal waves in his stare, I knew that I would take him with me, that I would drag him down, down to the cavern where I hid all my mistakes, to the cavity where I dressed my trophies with shells.

Monday Night Addict

I never thought that I would have the courage to speak to you, and now that I have, I wish I would have stitched my mouth shut. I almost walked away—in fact, one or two times I actually did—but now I'm left at the bar, throwing back Jack and scribbling my signature on a bar tab that is twice what I normally pay. I haven't spoken in months, don't plan on it anytime soon. Maybe if I quit using my vocal chords completely, the booze will eat through my throat. That way I can't say your name, can't scream it, yell it, or cry it in my sleep. That way I'm mute. Silent. Just a face in the bar.

MONSTER, ME

Inside of me, there's a sickness. A darkness that breeds and snuffs out the good, filling me with screams and cobwebs and an emptiness that infects everything that was once alive. It's a slow death and I feel everything: every touch, every kiss, every parting. Sometimes I even think my heart stops beating; it just quiets and goes kind of still, barely pulsing until it's not. I know it's her, and I know she holds me tighter than any lover I've ever known, and I hate her—*but oh do I love her*—and no matter how hard I try to fight, how desperately I try not to give in, she's always there, waiting, ready, and willing to take me as I am. Broken. Tired. Weak. She loves and accepts the tragedy of my being and she understands the cuts and the bruises, the stitches and the scars.

I call her monster and she moves within me, finding her comfort spot where she nestles down deep until her arms are mine, until my legs are hers. I see through two pairs of eyes, and breathe with four lungs, and the disease that breeds in my stomach is not a cancer of the flesh, but a mutation of the heart. She's the cure to my epidemic, my anti-suicide machine, and together we/I walk through this life, holding hands and hearts, whispering secrets and drinking down poisons, mixing black magic remedies and sucking down sage, and together we/I live, somehow we/I survive. My monster, me. The Jekyll to my Hyde.

Moral Wreckage

Sometimes you think things are going to go one way
and then they jar off to the right, swerve to the left
and then you're lost in a field in the middle of nowhere
trying to restart your morals with nothing more than an
idea of what you thought was going to happen—what
you were sure was going to happen—but what didn't and
never would.

MOURNING SEASON

Love.

It always feels the same and it never changes, no matter how many years pass, or how many times her heart gets broken.

It's blank, encompassing, and it kills her from the inside out as if it were some parasite drinking from her sadness until there was nothing left but to beg for death. Some people can get up and keep walking, keep going through their normal routine, but not her. Never her. She dies a bit each time she loves someone, and every time she watches them leave, leave like summer changing into fall, the hole in her chest gets deeper, spreads a little wider as it eats at the organ until there's nothing left but a walking corpse, a girl who only knows of winter, never of spring.

Murder and Merlot

There was a corkscrew on the nightstand, a late night treat for alcoholism and self-hatred and she picked it up, fingered the metallic curls, and licked off the aftertaste of merlot and bad memories. He was asleep and he was beautiful, and she hated herself, hated him for *making* her hate herself and there was a countdown in her head and it sang the songs she wished he would have sung to her and when she leaned over to kiss him—when she buried the corkscrew in his side, *over and over again*—it was the first time she felt something, something like love, and the blood on his lips tasted better than any fine wine he could have poured down her throat.

MUSIC MAN

He had a guitar and his music picked at the strings to her memory. She hated the song, hated the melody but every night at 4:15, she'd wake up to the sound of his playing even though he wasn't there, even though he never really was. She was in tune—in love—with an illusion, chasing after a lie, and when she'd wake up in the morning, she'd pour two cups of coffee, one for herself, and one for the musician in her head who wouldn't stop playing.

Napping in the Circles

Beelzebub whipped me awake,
but I couldn't help myself,
and despite the pain, I drifted off again,
a sloth in life, a sloth in death
sleep would always be my sin.

NEVER BELIEVE YOUR MEMORIES

The tricky part about memories is that they are only skeletons of the truth, little pieces of imperfections without muscle or tissue, without nerves or heart. They become stories that we tell ourselves, slivers of fiction that we read over and over as a way to defend ourselves against ourselves, and it's safer that way, to live in a fantasy, to remember what we think happened rather than relive what really did, and so let us sleep tonight, drunk on fairytales and daydreams knowing that our minds are eating away our nightmares, carefully devouring and hiding our pain.

No Longer Christian

I hide it well, but I'm a walking sin,
a gluttonous whore,
an envious bitch;
I drink myself to sleep,
lie myself out of situations,
out of greed, out of envy,
and the drugs,
the drugs keep me sane,
keep me normal, keep me fake,
and it's the only way I've learned
to survive, because being Christian
did nothing but *kill* the person I used to be.

NO MORE ANGELS

Break off her wings.
She doesn't deserve them;
monsters rarely do.

The Devil has a journal and in it he writes the names of people that have wronged me, people who deserve the circles, deserve the rage, and I think it's flattering that he lets me be the messenger, the harbinger of bad news, because there's nothing quite like seeing the look on your face when I'm the one handing you your death card, when I'm the one standing there with the Lord of Flies, smiling as we kiss, laughing as we scratch your life out of the book.

NUMBERING OUR SINS

In our house, Sundays were meant for solitude,
for personal reflection of sin;
Father said they were created to teach us regret,
to instill in us the power of guilt
and if we could count how we'd upset God
on both hands that week, we were allowed
to have extra souls for dinner that night.

Old Habits

I've always taken my whiskey straight and my men mean
but I'm getting to a point where the burn is starting to hurt
and the bruises aren't going away, so maybe I'll switch to
something a little lighter, something a lady
would drink, and maybe I'll flirt with manners and good intentions
instead of seeking out dirty stories and double shots at the bar.

ONLY HE CAN MAKE ME CRY

Breathe into me, wake next to me, just prove to me that I'm alive,
that I'm not some female corpse without purpose,
without cause. Let me hear your voice as I fall asleep,
feel the tickle of your hair against my cheek as I toss
and turn. I want your warmth on my skin, the sound
of your beating heart in my ears, and when the numbness
takes me, when the pain freezes in my eyes, I want to taste
your lips against mine, feel your tongue in my mouth, no,
I don't want the pills, I don't want the treatments. No more
appointments, no more doctors. The only sickness in my head is
there from when you went away, and sometimes if I close my eyes
hard enough, if I black out the world around me, I can almost see you,
almost smell the cigarettes on your breath, hear the rasp in your voice,
and it's in that moment, that brief break in time, that when I cut myself
I bleed, that when I see your brown eyes, I can cry.

Opium Den

Lights dim, flying high, I took a deep breath.
Inhale, baby. Hold it nice and strong.
I let the smoke and the sound of his voice collect in my lungs.
That's it, easy girl.
My head spun in circles and I started to drift.
Just give me your hand and let it all go.
I felt my body melt, felt my worries fade away.
Now exhale, baby. Exhale and kiss me goodbye.

ORDINARY WOMEN

Ordinary women are
dangerous;
they are the epitome,
the definition,
the classification
of the underestimated
and that is what makes them
unsafe.

Unsafe,
because no one expects an
ordinary woman to
stab her boyfriend in
the throat, to castrate him
with gardening shearers,
or set the house on fire when he sleeps.

Ordinary women
are a hazard, a loose cannon
of psychopathy waiting
for the precise moment
to go off, because ordinary
is camouflage and that's
what makes them a
threat.

Orphan

Alone is what I am,
separated, away from the pack, from what I knew
and there's a freedom to the betrayal,
a solace in the isolation. I didn't think I could
survive by myself, but after all those nights
spent sleeping under the stars, under the hate,
I've realized that being alone is what I needed
in order to be reborn, what I needed to experience
in order to come back, to be stronger than before.

PAIN AND PLEASURE, HEAVEN AND HELL

He was pain and he was pleasure and most times when he touched me I didn't know if I should scream or sigh. He was knives and petals, pins and feathers and he was a high unlike any other—a sadomasochistic dance of pure dread and utmost anticipation. I wanted to be nowhere near him, yet never away from his side, drawn to him like maggots were to death. I would writhe in his presence, body moving, mind racing, heart lost somewhere between Heaven and Hell and at the end of the night when he'd leave and I'd curl up inside myself, half-dead yet more alive than ever before. I knew he was my downfall, my punishment and my muse, and I knew that no matter when—or even how bad—I wanted things to stop, that I was powerless against him. He had me, controlled me, and he'd continue to do so until the death of my days, until the moment he took the last breath, because I was his, bound and broken, submissive and ever at his call.

I've noticed lately that when I'm driving, my mind kind of blanks out, kind of goes black, and I'm drifting, drifting on the road, drifting through life and I don't even have the energy to light my cigarette, so it just hangs out of my mouth as the taste of nicotine sits on my tongue, reminding me of how you used to taste, how you used to kiss me when you'd had too much wine and didn't know what you were doing, and part of me misses the uncertainty in the way you used hold me, part of me misses the way you used to look at me all scared and unsure, how you'd whisper 'you're beautiful' as if it was the most terrifying thing you'd ever said, and I've missed my street twice now thinking about you, thinking about your lips and the softness of the words you left me with, and I wonder where you are and if you're driving, if you're missing roads and running stop signs, if you're watching the stars and staying up till dawn so you can watch the darkness fade away and I've noticed lately that when I'm driving, that the music doesn't sound the same without you, that the car feels kind of empty, and the passenger seat sometimes screams.

PICNIC OF MOTHS

There were moths everywhere
—big ones, beautiful ones—
black white and gray, and they sat on my arms and shoulders as if I were a
tree branch. I could hear them talking, whispering to each other in their own
language, a sort of talk they didn't think that I could understand, but I used
to have wings once, too, and I knew what it was like to think that you were
special, to think that you were different, that you were safe.

They flew next to my cheek
—sat on my lips like a lover's kiss—
and I opened my mouth to let them collect on my tongue. They tasted like
rain, like forest, and I wanted to keep them inside me. I envied them, them
with their ability to leave, to fly away and touch the sky on whim. They were
cumulus, they were stars, and I swallowed them in groups, savoring the taste
of what I faintly recalled to be freedom.

I put the belt around my arm and slapped my veins. It was cold outside and the snow made my blood look blue, blue like his eyes, blue like my mood. I don't know when it all started and I don't know when—or *if*—I'll let it end, but for right now, right in this moment, this is the only way I know how to pray, this is my higher power, the way I talk to my God.

PLEASE, BREAK MY HEART

She wasn't living in a fantasy world; she knew he didn't love her, knew that it was all a play, a theatrical performance to satisfy some need that he buried deep down inside himself, so when she looked in the mirror day after day and asked herself why she put up with it, why she let the charades go on, there was only one answer that made sense:

she was a masochist,
and Christ, did she love the pain.

I've locked her away;
sometimes she screams
but mostly, she's quiet because she knows,
knows that as long as she's hidden, she's safe.
But there are those rare occasions when her heart is touched,
when she gets the urge to be again,
and I question her want to interact with others,
with people and situations who can break her again, but he seemed different,
like someone we could both trust,
so I let her out, just for a taste,
just for a little bite
to see if he could satisfy all those wants,
if he could satiate all her needs.

PUNCTURE WOUNDS

People think they're special when they get the circles, when they get the marks, but what they really are is stupid. No divine intervention is coming for you, no supernatural stigmata is happening. If I stab myself four times in the right places, I'm not going to heaven. Trust me, I know. I've tried. And now I'm in Hell for suicide. So stitch yourself up and stop praying. Only one man survives the cross and no matter how much blood you lose, you're still not impressing anyone but the big guy below.

Queen of Spades

Feminine royalty
dressed to kill,
she carries a shovel
to her coronation
to bury her dead.

QUEST TO QUIET

I need to quiet your voice,
I have to take your whispers—
your mouth, the movement of your lips—
off repeat because *'I love you, girl'* has kept me wading through purgatory,
through endless hurt and passionate emptiness for six restless months,
and whether it be fire or air
I just need to burn
burn or fly
fly, fly away.

Did you love him, or did you just tell yourself that you did in order to live out some fantasy, some make-believe moments where your life didn't seem so empty, so broken? When you kissed him, did you feel breathless or did you feel the wet slap of lips, the moist puckering of chapped skin and bleeding gums? When you touched him, did you feel safe or were you just waiting for the climax of danger to build up until it destroyed you completely?

Did you care that you were dying?
Did you notice it at all?

Did you sleep well at night, curled up in his embrace, or were you alone on the other side of the bed, riding the draft as it raped you repeatedly until the sun broke through the clouds? Did you ever kiss him when you woke up, or were you too afraid to get close to him, too nervous that your words might meet his fist?

Did you care that you deserved better?
Did you believe in yourself at all?

Did you realize that he didn't touch you, that he treated you like you were diseased, like you were some leper, some tainted whore that didn't deserve his attention or his lust? When you came home at night, were you ever greeted with excitement or were you only ever met with despair, disappointment? Was there ever a moment when you felt good, when you felt whole, or were you drowning in a home of neglect, a sea of narcissism and lies?

Did you care that you were worthy of more?
Did you love yourself at all?

Because now you're bloated and blue here on this metal slab, lost in some black hole, some nightmare that I can't bring you back from, some death that's fixed itself permanently to your face, to your smile, to your eyes, eyes that are closed, but still crying, and I can't find you anymore, can't hear you anymore, and it's hard to think that love brought you here, that too much faith in someone finally put you on my table, finally brought you to my morgue.

Quick Fix

Your absence is painful even though I still feel you beside me, and when I wake up and don't see you, don't hear from you, it's like I'm swallowing razor blades to get the silence out of my throat. I wish it didn't end like this with all the drugs and the booze and the ashes—*Christ, there were so many ashes*—and I wonder what you're doing when the sun goes down, if the thought of me, of us, even crosses your mind, but I want you to know that your face is all that I dream and the memory of your voice is what sings me to sleep, and regardless of where you are, or who you're with, you're the fix that I need to get me through the day, the tragedy that keeps me writing, that keeps me hoping, wishing that this is all some lie and that one day, I won't have to rely on just memories of you, that one day, you'll be with me while I'm writing about love, about happiness, about Heaven instead of Hell.

RAIN CLOUD IN HER EYES

It was in that moment—the moment when she sat in her car in silence, when she choked on the mascara and wet lipstick that dribbled into her mouth—that she realized that she'd given all of herself away, that she was broken, unfixable. She knew that there was no one, not even herself that could put her back together again and when she looked in the rearview mirror, there were nothing but storms brewing in her eyes, eyes that were dressed in two overcast clouds accessorized with the destruction of thunder and rain. They'd gone black and absent and when she closed them, there was lightning in her head and it struck her hard, brought her forehead against the steering wheel. She didn't flinch when she hit the tree, didn't even budge. Her blood became a blanket and it kept her warm throughout the night, warm in a way that she'd never experienced from any man, nor any lover. She thought about staying there, there amongst the broken limbs and crumbled leaves. The constellations and busted headlights. Yes, she thought about staying there, there where she would be at peace; a wreck amongst a wreck, two parts of the same whole, both destroyed and beyond repair. No one would judge her. Not there. Not in the car, the car that held her—trapped her—tighter than any arms that ever held her, than the hands that she was used to being fixed around her throat.

It's strange to think that we were once lovers,
that at one point in time,
no matter the second,
no matter the day,
your existence in my life
was the only truth that mattered.

REPOSSESSION

An eye for an eye, a tooth for a tooth,
scripture created the principles of revenge,
a caveat to thievery as repossession
as human harvest
became justified.
Respectfully, 666

People always ask me how to get into Heaven,
and I tell them I don't know, I've never been,
but this side of 666 is delightful, and the weather
is always warm.

Sleeping was impossible and being awake wasn't an option either, not with him around, not with him alive. The very idea of him—of his very existence—made the hole in my chest darken, made it grow deeper by the second. It hurt too much to see him, even if it was only in my head, and I threw up every morning from the venom of his memory, cried myself raw at night until I sobbed my way into a void. My body withered, shedding weight as I starved myself in order to feel something, something other than the encroaching loss that ate at me throughout the day. I didn't know what else to do; I had no idea where he was, and if I saw him, I didn't think I was strong enough to go through with it, to actually *do* it.

So I waited.
Waited a week, two, maybe three.

And when it was obvious that he was never coming back—when I was certain that it was over—I made up my mind to silence his voice, to carve his memory out of my heart. I took the blade and pushed it into my sternum, cut a little line down my navel and watched it bleed nightmares and darkness, poison and pain. Black and gray swirls crawled out of my chest like a winter fog, screaming, howling, and I smiled, smiled nice and big as I bled heartache all over my bed. My sheets were red and I was white, white with death, with happiness, with purity, but most importantly I was numb and I didn't—couldn't—see him anymore.

ROGUE SOULS

Wanderers they were, the beaten and the bruised,
the unloved and the unwanted; my spirit called to them,
sought them out unbeknownst to me, and they answered,
welcoming the invitation with their laughter and their howls.

I was dead, you see—
dead of heart and dead of mind,
and it was my decay that fed their hunger,
that satiated their thirst.

It was no surprise that they followed me home that night,
always present, always near,
and when I crawled into my bed,
they were waiting beneath the sheets,
beneath my innocence,
their hands cold against my stomach,
their tongues coarse on my neck
and I shivered as they held me,
as they kissed me,
for they were the rogue, the lost,
the quiet ones looking for someone,
someone to harvest, someone to claim.

Self-Lobotomy

Sometimes the best defense is to forget, to just wipe your memory clean and start over again. A blank slate. Innocence. It sounds good on paper, but then again, so did I. And yet, here I am, staring at the walls and waiting for them to collapse. There's no shame in giving up; in fact, sometimes that's the harder thing to do, to just quit, to stop believing in someone, to stop having faith in yourself. There are some people that can't be fixed, and now I know I'm one of them. Maybe someday I won't remember. Maybe this stick will make it all just go away.

SHADES OF BLACK AND BLUE

I was innocent, but he was a sadist and I had no idea what I'd gotten myself into, what I was already letting happen even as my body started to change colors, started to break. From porcelain to black, from milk to purple, I transformed into a human punching bag as he beat me every night, as he loved me the only way he knew how. Some women shirk from the violence, some ladies get off. I don't know which one I was; I was barely a woman, and I was never a lady. And he bit me, grabbed me, and his teeth marks and fingerprints dressed my neckline, my stomach, my thighs. I didn't try to hide it, in fact I wore it as a prize, as a series of love notes carefully written into my flesh, as a song we both shared, each crescendo my screams, each drop my sighs.

Stay Buried

Resurrection isn't for everyone;
sometimes it's better to stay underground
where you belong.

STILETTOS AND ROOFTOPS

A pair of my stilettos were left hanging on the telephone wire last night, and I'm not proud of how they got there—*just kidding, of course I am*— because it takes a lot of effort to lure a man on top of a building, but then again, not as much as one might think. I climbed the fire escape with ease despite being half-drunk and in five inch heels, and when I click-clacked onto the roof, I laid down, my dress hiked up past my thighs as I called for him to join me. I kicked my legs in the air like Marilyn Monroe and sent my black beauties flying, soaring through the air as they wrapped themselves around that thin electric line that seemed to be carefully etched in space. I lost a lot of things that night—my morals included—but at least I knew where to find my shoes when I woke up.

Your voice sounds like a song that's asking me to disappear and I can't help but listen to it, can't help but obey. Every time I watch your lips form my name, a part of me flickers like static on the television screen. I feel myself lessening, evaporating off the ground like the steam from your morning coffee.

...

...

...

And there's this spark in my eye, an orb of absence and while I'm blind, I can still hear, still hear my body folding in on itself, wrapping itself up like a hand-me-down gift dressed in used tissue paper. My backbone has been shattered, my spine…it's obsolete. And there's a quiet death in my chest as your words flow through an empty rib cage, greeting acid and worry as they travel down my core.

...

...

...

I am no longer someone, no longer female, no longer human. I am but a hologram, a vision of the person who I used to be, a mirage of the body that I used to have before I met you, you who sealed me up, who took away everything that I had: bone, flesh, blood, who left me with nothing but shadows, shadows and suffering, and now all I can do is wait, wait to be subtracted, wait to be erased.

...

...

xxx

THAT ONE OCTOBER NIGHT

I wake up and see you in the memories I refuse to delete because I still want to see you make coffee every day and I don't want to forget the way you slept, the way you'd smile yourself awake and burrow into my arms. I can still taste your kiss if I concentrate hard enough, and no matter how many tears I've cried, my visions of you are sweet, sweet like the day I first tasted wine on your lips, beautiful like the afternoons we spent messing up beds in hotel suites, perfect like the nights we walked in back alleys, hand in hand, breaking into abandoned houses and sleeping on wooden floors. I needed nothing when I was with you, nothing but your love, and that was pure, regardless of the pain, and so I'll carry you with me, forever in heart, always in mind, because when I was with you, time as I knew it stood still; the world, the night, my breath, it all simply—and perfectly—stopped.

The Devil's Shadow

He created me like a shadow, something dark, something permanent and once he put his lips on me, I couldn't escape. I've since kissed pages with his name as I've walked through this nightmare, a silhouette that falls behind but never leaves his side as my punishment for his love is purgatory, a blinding repetition where I wake when he sleeps and our only conversations are whispers caught between dreams. My heart is a prison overrun by his demons, my mind a silent film, and when he moves, I mimic him, a pathetic desperation to remember what it felt like to walk with him, beside him, hand in hand, instead of trailing behind like a lost memory, like a discarded doll and yet when he looks for me, I sink into the floorboards like a pool of ink, afraid to show myself, ashamed that this is what love has turned me into but not too ashamed that I'm ready to walk away.

THE DREAM BUTCHER

I don't want to believe the man outside my window, but I can't pretend that what he's telling me isn't true. You killed them, didn't you? Every last one of them, and you're not even sorry. I can tell by the look on your face and it doesn't bother you that my voice is cracking, or that there are tears streaming hot down my cheeks. Tell me, please. Did none of them survive? Not even the babies, the ones that had barely began to grow?

The man outside is calling you a butcher, a madman with a knife, and I have to think, I have to believe that you're inhuman, that you must be something other than the flesh and blood that runs within man in order to do something like this, especially to me, me the girl you said you'd always love, the girl you said you'd never hurt. We were lovers, we were friends, we were souls intertwined and I trusted you and I believed in you and I gave you my heart and my mind and my body and you strangled them—my rainy-day children, my summer-night kids—you strangled them while I slept, snuffed them out while I slumbered so that I wouldn't notice that they'd gone quiet, so that I wouldn't notice that they weren't just bleeding but rather already dead.

The Girl Who Slept With Monsters

She's a sweet girl, a quiet girl, a girl you'd never expect to sleep with monsters, to sleep with men, men that bite, that cut, that stab, and she hugs their claws and kisses their fangs, trying to tame the creatures within, but she's a dumb girl, a stupid girl, and she doesn't realize that you can't win over a beast without shedding a little blood. But still she tries, and she dies, and she dies and eventually she stops getting up, stops trying to win because the pain in her heart, in her eyes, in her smile was too much to fake and that sweet girl, that quiet girl, that girl you'd never expect, fed her heart to the men, to the monsters as she climbed into her grave and slept herself to death.

THERE'S A CORPSE IN MY MIRROR

There's a corpse in my mirror, but no one else
can see him but me. The rest of you, the watchers,
the wishers, you don't walk with the moonlight
like we do. You don't howl at the stars and count the
years like we do, and I was lost for so long, buried amongst
you—the living!—walking around like a bag of hot flesh when
the chill I'd been looking for, when the *death* I'd been
searching for was six feet beneath the very spot where I
stand. He wasn't always there, wasn't
always lingering in my reflection, standing behind me,
in front of me, next to me, *inside of me*, but there's no
denying him now. It's been too long and I'm as much
a part of him as he is of me. We're two halves to the whole
and I'm the Eve to his Adam, the apple to the snake, bound
by blood, by bite, by teeth, and I wear his mark on my neck
like a crimson choker fashioned by the kiss of an Iron Maiden,
so all of you—the meat sacks, the blood baskets, the skin suits—know
that I'm taken, know that I'm real and know that this time,
I'm very much alive.

Thought Process

And so she asked herself
what am I getting out of this?
and the answer was simple:
pain.

TORTURE TATTOOS

The angel knew what she was doing, knew how to play the game, and she branded her men and women well, took ink and fire to their skin, marked them like cattle; if they wanted to earn their wings they'd have to prove it by removing their flesh, by shearing off the stained canvas of their past, and then, and only then, could they shed their skin like snakes, like serpents who knew which apple to bite, which Eden to destroy.

Ugly Patterns

There were times when I fell asleep next to you wondering if I'd wake up the next day and see you lying there next to me, dead and pale, drowned in your drugs, in your booze, in your self-hate. Sometimes I wondered if I was safe, if even I would wake up, but those feelings were just fear because I knew you'd never hurt me and I don't know a lot about love, and there's a lot more I don't understand about you, but if I learned anything from those days, those nights, it was that I'm stronger than I thought, but that I'm weaker, too.

UMBRELLA THE RAIN

Sometimes I wonder if I willingly walk into storms,
or if I just bring the thunder with me, if I just umbrella
the rain, because there's always this darkness, this lightning, and it reflects in
my eyes, in my heart, and in my soul as it electrocutes the small
rays of sun left over from whatever happiness I used to feel, and
now there's nothing—*nothing!*—left but a gray cloud in a drab sky that paints
sadness in the air, washes pain in the wind, and the broken promises
that lay on the train tracks, the broken hearts that linger in the
trees, they speak to me in whispers, pleading, screaming, begging, and I
cry and I cry and I die and I die and when the hurricane in my head
is done raging, when the tornado in my chest is done destroying,
I sit there in the puddle of some stranger's tears
and let myself drown in what's left of the night.

Under the Alter

Cloaked in daggers,
he slipped me a note in the hallway,
told me to be on my back in 15 minutes
to be under the alter,
hidden from the cross—
from the eyes of the envious—
and that we would be together
together in sin,
in the only way we knew
to worship our God

UNKNOWN MAN

Everyone warned me, said I was too far in, too much involved that I couldn't see clearly anymore, but I couldn't help it; I was obsessed, infatuated and divine possession took over me as the ecstasies of heaven rained through my eyes, through my chest in holy rage. I wanted nothing more than to change my past, to change my present, and a man in a black garb told me that he could help, told me that he could turn back time and wash away the sins that had collected on my hands like dust in an attic. His words were soft, lyrical, and I listened to him whisper, listened to him sing as he filled my head with lies, with promises he had no intention of keeping, and I followed him into the shadows, ran after him while everyone screamed, and I don't know that anyone will ever find me now as no one thinks to look for the missing in Hell.

Unlucky Seven

I roll a solid seven every time;
one for each sin that landed me here,
and now no one will partner with me
because I always collect the most debt.

VACCINATING VIRGIL

The poet had a rough job,
yet poets usually do,
and after escorting Dante through all that filth,
there weren't enough showers in the world
to cleanse him of what he saw.

Verisimilitude

The appearance of being real or true looked similar to the way your name rested on my lips when I tried to conjure you at night; it sounded a lot like forever, a single circle of love and destruction, an act of lust, a performance of hate and when I closed my eyes to the image of you that I held in my memory, the one that floats somewhere in that cold October night, I wonder if I ever met you, if I ever loved you, or if you were just a mirage, a mist, a face in a bar, a face in a crowd and I hope someday that I'll get to see you again, really see you, and then maybe the poetry in my head will rewrite itself something new, something happier than what's already written down, a new ending for a newly broken circle, a shape that's more than what it originally appeared to be.

VICTIM OF THE VEIL

Everyone thinks it's funny to point and laugh at the people who are different, at the people who see things that others can't, that others refuse to open their eyes to. But not all of us were born without veils, given the ability to see a world of fantasy rather than the reality that lurks around us. If I could choose not to see the dead, I would welcome a moment of sanity, but I'm not that lucky, and so I watch them every day, staring at me, beckoning me as they move through time, through a plane that isn't their own. They are trapped and I am victim, forced to see them, but unable to help.

So go ahead and laugh.
I'm not alone.
I'll always have them with me.

Vindication

The night I saw the Devil,
he was looking at me through your eyes,
through the man I'd grown to love,
to cherish and adore,
but that man was gone,
and in his place was someone I didn't recognize,
something much, much worse.

VISIONS

Today is a hallucinogenic mystery
and I'm seeing double,
hearing voices I've never heard,
and I'm blooming in neon colors
as I bid this moment goodbye.

What Waits in the Elevator Shaft

For Nathan

When she closed her eyes, she could see it, and if she focused hard enough, she could hear it, too. It lived in the walls and it slept next to her at night, scratching at the plaster as it tried to get closer to her. Sometimes she'd hear it cry, soft wails echoing down through the floors, but other times it would scream, blood-curdling and mad, ripping at the lock to try and get out, to try and get to her. No one believed her when she said she felt its breath on her at night, that she felt it stare at her through the cracks in the wood, but when her bruises started to darken, when the handprints started to emerge, the other people in the house began to second guess the girl's crazy, the other people began to believe.

Tap...
  Tap...
    Tap...

She still slept in the room, afraid that if she left, that if she tried to get away that the thing would only follow her, would only get worse. She started to sleep with the lights on, but that only made it mad. It wanted darkness, the darkness of the night, the darkness of her soul, and when the light bulbs burned bright, the thing would bang against the walls, pounding its fists, kicking its feet and throwing tantrums like a six-year-old child, and a child she knew it was because lately when it whispered to her, lately when it visited her at night, it held her and called her mom, cuddled up next to her—blackened and bathed in an age-old must—and begged to be let out of its cage, to be free once and for all.

Tap...
  Tap...
    Tap...

The lines between dream and reality faded fast, and the girl hugged the thing back, afraid of what would happen if she didn't, afraid that part of her wanted to hold it all along. The thing—boy? girl?—was wet and smelled like well-water, smelled like death, and she didn't know how to free it, how to bring it back, so she just held it tighter and listened to it wheeze, held it as it shook, and when dawn peeked in through her windows the next morning, there was nothing but silence in the room, but a subtle scratching in her chest.

AN EXORCISM

White Lines

Your cocaine eyes gave me chills,
the kind of chills that got into my veins,
turned them blue,
and froze me from the inside out,
and I wonder if things would have been
different if I would have just tried the wine
leftover on your lips, but the way you looked
at me that night—like I was the only person in the world—
made me weak, weak enough to
try you, curious enough to take you in.

WHITE NOISE

Shackled to her conscience, she couldn't walk away, couldn't let herself run. There was something holding her back, something pressing, something very much like guilt and it ate away at her, preventing her from moving on, from living any kind of life. Pain became a constant, an ever-present state of mind, and the girl didn't know what it felt like to have her thoughts be at peace. All she knew was screaming and the voices weren't even real, they were more like white noise, like brief stabs of electricity that shocked her full of shame. She tried everything to silence them, but no matter how far she crawled into her head, how deep she dug into her ears, there was never anything that came out, nothing except blood, blood and bad memories.

And then the voices just grew louder.

She'd rest her head at night and fill her pillow with whispers and prayers, prayers she knew would never be answered, whispers she knew would never be heard. There were moments when she'd cry, but they were few because the voices would only leak out her eyes and lick up her tears. They'd mock her, disgrace her, guilt her for not being strong enough, for not being the one person that could handle everything they had to say. And on the off chance that sleep would take her, they'd write out the outline to her dreams, the dialogue to her nightmares, taking away any chance she had for quiet, any chance she had to put them on mute.

Womb Therapy

He told me that in order to start over I had to go back to darkness, back to rebirth, so I laid down on the metal slab, my identity curled beneath me, and I let him push me into the drawer like I was some corpse, some product for inventory. The morgue was quiet and I couldn't hear anything but my own breathing, couldn't see anything but the reel of images and memories that crowded the closed space as I screamed in the box. My head turned claustrophobic and I couldn't tell what was real or how long I'd been in there—days, weeks, years?—and when the door cracked open, and the light blinded my eyes, I had no idea who or what I was, I only knew that inside was safe, that alone was safe, and that I didn't want to leave.

XOXO

I signed my letters with hugs and straightjackets,
with kisses and bites,
and sometimes I'd seal the envelope
with the spit from your name;
a thank-you note of curses,
a love-letter hex.

Yanking Teeth

He wore teeth like a necklace,
pushed them deep into skin
and I wanted to be among them,
somewhere close to his heart
in a pearl-white design; so I smiled at him,
spellbound by his silver hooks,
and every part of me wanted those razors
to slash my tongue,
to bleed me bloody
to take me like no man ever did
and keep me like no man
ever could.

YEARNING FOR COMPANIONSHIP

I touched him,
touched him against my better judgment,
and he was soft,
warm,
but then again,
so was I,
and I was the coldest person
I knew.

I am dead, of that I am certain and of that I accept; I cry no tears for my death, but plenty of memories linger in what's left of the conscious thoughts that I still form. I know now I shouldn't have loved him, shouldn't have given him my heart. It was the one possession that I kept hidden from so many for so long, and once it was gone, I had nothing left to offer but my soul, a price that I didn't I think I would have to pay for so soon. For some women, falling in love is beautiful, but for others, others like me—the broken, the beaten and the bruised—love is not a fairytale and it's not a game. When I fell in love with him, I fell in want, in desire, in lust. I wanted him and his dreams, his longings, I wanted to bring him every pleasure and every happiness but love is defined differently by every person, and to him, love was a prison not an escape. He took my body on his terms, not with love but with greed, with a selfishness that made me want to peel off my skin and wrap myself in shame. I felt sin crawl into bed with me at night, wrap its arms around me while I slept. I cried more than I smiled, was silent more than I laughed, and now as I look at my body, buried in the insulation of the attic, I know that even knowing what I know now, that given a second chance, I wouldn't have done anything different, wouldn't have been able to if I tried, because in that moment when my lips first brushed against his, I knew that I would have given my last breath to have a chance at getting his heart in return, given my last day if I could wake up in his arms. And so here I am, true to my word, lost amongst the rafters, a ghost of the woman I could have been, should have been, a slave to the man I only ever wanted to love but who refused to love me back.

ZOMBIE

The light makes me cringe but I'm sick of being underground, tired of being dead and alone, and the earth smells so good, so fresh, so inviting, that I'm tempted to claw my way out, to swallow the maggots breeding in-between my teeth and take a breath of fresh air. There's something to be said for the living, something to note about the rush of blood in their cheeks, and every once in a while I catch myself doing this—watching them like they're something to be envied—but then I remember all the days I spent watching the people like me, remember all the nights where it hurt too much to live, and that's when I crawl back in the grave, back below the surface, where the worms keep me warm and the dirt keeps me sane.

AN EXORCISM

Zzzz

I'm tired,
tired of waking up,
exhausted from sleeping,
but the sloth in me wants to crawl back in bed,
to hide beneath the covers,
to drown in pillows and sweat,
but the other part of me—the part that believes that people can change—
wants to stay awake,
to take a shot at life, at living,
at trying to be real again even though I'm already
half-asleep, lost between fact and fiction, between dream and reality,
and no one can hurt me when I'm asleep,
when I'm wrapped in my safety-net,
hidden away from the world
and while it's nice to fantasize
I know this is where I belong.

ABOUT THE AUTHOR

Stephanie M. Wytovich is the Poetry Editor for Raw Dog Screaming Press, a book reviewer for *Nameless Magazine*, and a well-known coffee addict. She is a member of the Science Fiction Poetry Association and a graduate from Seton Hill University's MFA program for Writing Popular Fiction. Her Bram Stoker Award nominated poetry collections *HYSTERIA: A Collection of Madness* and *Mourning Jewelry* can be found at www.rawdogscreaming.com, and Wytovich's debut novel, *The Eighth*, is due out in 2015 from Dark Regions Press. Follow her at stephaniewytovich.blogspot.com and on twitter @JustAfterSunset.

www.ingramcontent.com/pod-product-compliance
Lightning Source LLC
LaVergne TN
LVHW041155080426
835511LV00006B/615